'Happiness
beyond all words!
A life of peace
and love, entire
and whole!'

DANTE ALIGHIERI
Born 1265, Florence, Italy
Died 1321, Ravenna, Italy

Dante wrote the *Divina Commedia* between 1308 and 1321.
This selection of cantos is taken from *Paradiso* translated by
Robin Kirkpatrick, Penguin Classics, 2007.

DANTE IN PENGUIN CLASSICS

Inferno
Purgatorio
Paradiso
The Divine Comedy
Vita Nuova

DANTE ALIGHIERI

Love that moves the sun and other stars

Translated by
Robin Kirkpatrick

PENGUIN BOOKS

PENGUIN CLASSICS

UK | USA | Canada | Ireland | Australia
India | New Zealand | South Africa

Penguin Classics is part of the Penguin Random House group of companies
whose addresses can be found at global.penguinrandomhouse.com.

This selection first published in Penguin Classics 2016

014

Translation copyright © Robin Kirkpatrick, 2007

The moral right of the author has been asserted

Set in 9/12.4 pt Baskerville 10 Pro
Typeset by Jouve (UK), Milton Keynes
Printed and bound in Great Britain by Clays Ltd, Elcograf S.p.A.

A CIP catalogue record for this book is available from the British Library

ISBN: 978-0-241-25042-6

www.greenpenguin.co.uk

Contents

Canto III

She – as the sun who first in love shone warm
into my heart – had now, by proof and counterproof,
disclosed to me the lovely face of truth.

And being ready, as was only right,
to own my errors – and new certainties –
I flung my head back, and I meant to speak.

But then, it seemed, a vision came to me
and bound me up so tightly to itself
that these confessions would not come to mind.

Compare: from clear and polished panes of glass,
or else from glinting waters, calm and still
(but not so deep their depths are lost in darkness),

we see reflections that reveal a hint,
though faint, of our own looks, and reach the eye
less strongly than a pearl on some white brow.

So I saw many faces, keen to speak,
and ran now to the opposite mistake
from that which fired the love of man and stream.

No sooner had I noticed – and supposed
that these were seemings in a looking-glass –
I turned my eyes to see who these might be.

I saw there nothing, so returned my glance
straight to the shining-out of my dear guide,
who, smiling at me, blazed in her own look.

'You baby!' she said. 'Don't worry or wonder,
to see me smile at all these ponderings.
Those feet are not yet steady on the ground of truth.

Your mind, from habit, turns round to a void.
And yet those beings that you see are true,
bound here below for vows they disavowed.

So speak to them. And hear and trust their words.
The light of truth that feeds them with its peace
will never let their feet be turned awry.'

Now turning to the shadow who most yearned,
in love and pure delight, to speak to me,
I said, nearly entranced by eagerness:

'You spirit, well created in the rays
of this eternity of life, you feel
a sweetness never known, if not by taste.

Let me, then, in your kindness, hear your name,
and tell me what your destiny has been.'
To which – eyes smiling – she at once replied:

'We, living in God's love, can no more lock
our doors against true-minded aims of will
than God's love does, which wills this court like him.

I was a virgin sister in the world.
Search deep in memory. My being now
more beautiful won't hide me from your eyes.

I am Piccarda – as you'll know I am –
and blessed among the many who are blessed,
within this slowest moving of the spheres.

The flames of what we feel are lit in us
by pleasure purely in the Holy Spirit,
dancing for happiness in that design.

And though the part allotted us may seem
far down, the reason is that, yes, we did
neglect our vows. These were in some part void.'

'A wonder shining in the look you have
reveals,' I said, 'an I-don't-know of holiness
that alters you from how you once were seen.

So recognition did not speed to mind.
Yet all you say has helped me understand.
Your image speaks precisely to me now.

But tell me this: you are so happy here,
have you no wish to gain some higher grade,
to see and be as friends to God still more?'

Smiling a moment with the other shades,
she then, in utmost happiness, replied,
blazing, it seemed, in the first fires of love:

'Dear brother, we in will are brought to rest
by power of *caritas* that makes us will
no more than what we have, nor thirst for more.

Were our desire to be more highly placed,
all our desires would then be out of tune
with His, who knows and wills where we should be.

Yet discord in these spheres cannot occur –
as you, if you reflect on this, will see –
since charity is *a priori* here.

In formal terms, our being in beatitude
entails in-holding to the will of God,
our own wills thus made one with the divine.

In us, therefore, there is, throughout this realm,
a placing, rung to rung, delighting all
– our king as well in-willing us in will.

In His volition is the peace we have.
That is the sea to which all being moves,
be it what that creates or Nature blends.'

3

Now it was clear. I saw that everywhere
in Paradise there's Heaven, though grace may rain
in varied measure from the Highest Good.

But then, as often happens over food
(though satisfied with one, we crave the next,
reaching for that while still we're saying 'thanks'),

so now in word and gesture I betrayed
an eagerness to hear from her what weave
her spool had not yet drawn out to the end.

'Perfect in life, her merits raised on high,
there is a lady – more in-heavened than we –
who wrote, on earth, a Rule of dress and veil,

that lets its wearer sleep and wake till death
beside a husband who accepts those vows
that charity conforms to his delight.

To follow her, I fled – a girl, no more –
out of the world. I pulled her cowl to me,
and promised my obedience to that Rule.

Men now arrived, more set on harm than good.
They dragged me from the cloister I had loved,
and God well knows what then my life became.

But, over to my right, there shows to you
another splendour who, enkindled now
with all the light that gathers in our sphere,

knows from her own life what I say of mine.
She was our sister. And from her head, too,
was torn the shadow of her pure, white hood.

This is the light of Constance, that high queen
who bore to Swabia's second storm a son,
the third – and ultimate – of that great line.

And yet – although against her will, against
all decency – she went back to the world,
she never let the veil fall from her heart.'

Those were her words to me. But then '*Ave
Maria*' began, singing. And, singing,
she went from sight, as weight sinks deep in water.

My eyes pursued as far as eyesight can,
but, as I lost her, so I turned once more
to target a desire far greater still.

Now all my thoughts were fixed on Beatrice.
But she, as lightning strikes, so stunned my gaze,
my eyes at first could not support the sight,

and this was why my question came so slow.

Canto X

Looking within his Son through that same Love
that Each breathes out eternally with Each,
the first and three-fold Worth, beyond all words,

formed all that spins through intellect or space
in such clear order it can never be,
that we, in wonder, fail to taste Him there.

Lift up your eyes, then, reader, and, along with
me, look to those wheels directed to that part
where motions – yearly and diurnal – clash.

And there, entranced, begin to view the skill
the Master demonstrates. Within Himself,
He loves it so, His looking never leaves.

Look! Where those orbits meet, there branches off
the slanting circles that the planets ride
to feed and fill the world that calls on them.

And were the path it takes not twisted so,
then many astral virtues would be wasted,
and almost all potential, down here, dead.

And were the distance any more or less
from that straight course, then much – above and here –
so ordered in the world, would be a void.

Now, reader, sit there at your lecture bench.
And, if you want not tedium but joy,
continue thinking of the sip you've had.

I've laid it out. Now feed on it yourself.
The theme of which I'm made to be scribe
drags in its own direction all my thoughts.

The greatest minister of natural life
who prints the worth of Heaven on the world,
and measures time for us in shining light,

conjoined with Aries (as we've called to mind),
was spinning through those spirals where, each hour,
its presence is revealed to us the sooner.

And with him I was there, but no more knew
of making that ascent than anyone
will know a thought before it first appears.

It's she – Beatrice – who sees the way,
from good to better still, so suddenly
her actions aren't stretched out in passing time.

How brilliant they must all, themselves, have been
seen in the sun where I now came to be,
not in mere hue but showing forth pure light.

Call as I might on training, art or wit,
no words of mine could make the image seen.
Belief, though, may conceive it, eyes still long.

In us, imagination is too mean
for such great heights. And that's no miracle.
For no eye ever went beyond the sun.

So shining there was that fourth family
that's always fed by one exalted Sire
with sight of what He breathes, what Son He has.

And now, 'Give thanks,' Beatrice began.
'Give thanks to the Him, the Sun of all the angels.
In grace, He's raised you to this sun of sense.'

No mortal heart was ever so well fed
to give itself devoutly to its God
so swiftly, with such gratitude and joy,

as now, to hear her words ring, I became.
I set my love so wholly on that Sun
that He, in oblivion, eclipsed even Beatrice.

This did not trouble her. She smiled at it.
And brightness from the laughter in her eyes
shared out to many things my one whole mind.

Bright beyond seeing, I saw, now, many flares
make us their centre and themselves our crown,
still sweeter even in voice than radiance.

Sometimes, in that same way, we see a zone
around Latona's daughter – lunar rays,
held in by gravid air, which form her belt,

There in that heavenly court from which I come
are found so many jewels, so fine, so rare,
they cannot be abstracted from that realm.

The singing of the lights was one of these.
So minds who don't, self-winged, coming flying here,
must wait to gather news from tongues struck mute.

And when, still singing, all these burning suns
had spun three turns around us where we were –
as stars more swift the closer to fixed poles –

girl-like in formal dance they looked to me,
in figure still but silent, pausing now,
listening until they caught the next new note.

And deep in one of these I heard begin: 'When
rays of grace igniting love in truth –
those rays through which, in loving, love still grows –

reflect in you so multiplied that you
are led along with them to climb this stair,
which none descends who will not rise again,

  whoever, seeing this, should then withhold
the wine flask that you thirst for counts as free
no more than rain *not* streaming to the ocean.

  You wish to know what plants these are – enflowered,
entranced – a garland round that *donna* who,
in beauty, strengthens you to dare the skies.

  I was a lamb within that holy flock
that Dominic conducts along the road
where "All grow fat who do not go astray".

  This one, who here is nearest on my right,
was master to me, and a brother, too –
Albert of Köln. I'm Thomas Aquinas.

  And if you wish to know the rest as well,
then follow with your eyes the words I speak,
circling around this interwoven string.

  The next flame blazes out from Gratian's smile.
He's loved in Paradise for having served
both civil and ecclesial courts so well.

  Then next, that Peter ornaments our choir
who, like the widow in Saint Luke's account,
offered his treasured all to Holy Church.

  The fifth light, and the loveliest of us all,
breathes with such love that everyone down there
hungers to have fresh word if he is saved.

  A mind so high is there, to which was sent
knowledge so deep that, if the truth is true,
no second ever rose who saw so much.

  You see a candle shining by him there
that saw, while in the flesh, most inwardly
the nature of the angels and their works.

Then in the very smallest of these lights
there smiles the one who spoke for Christian times.
Augustine cited him in what he wrote.

Now if, to track my words of praise, you draw
the eye of intellect from light to light,
already you'll be thirsting for the eighth.

Rejoicing, deep within, to see all good,
the blessèd soul is there who made quite plain
the world's fallaciousness – to all who'd hear.

The body he was driven from lies, now,
below in Golden Heaven Church. He came
to peace from exile, from his martyrdom.

Burning beyond, you see the breathing fires
of Bede, then Isidore and Richard, too –
in contemplation he was more than man.

The one from whom your glance returns to me
is light born of that spirit who, oppressed
in thought, saw death, it seemed, come all too slow.

This is the everlasting light of Siger,
whose lectures, given in Straw Alleyway,
argued for truths that won him envious hate.'

And now, like clocks that call us at the hour
in which the Bride of God will leave her bed
to win the Bridegroom's love with morning song,

where, working, one part drives, the other draws –
its 'ting-ting' sounding with so sweet a note
that now the spirit, well and ready, swells –

so in its glory I beheld that wheel
go moving round and answer, voice to voice,
tuned to a sweetness that cannot be known,

except up there where joy in-evers all.

Canto XI

Those idiotic strivings of the human mind!
How flawed their arguments and logic are,
driving our wings to flap in downward flight.

Some follow Law. Some drift (great tomes in hand)
to Medicine, others train in priestly craft.
Some rule by force, as others do by tricks.

Some choose to steal, some trade in politics,
some toil, engrossed in pleasures of the flesh,
and others concentrate their minds on ease,

while I, released from all that sort of thing,
was gathered up on high with Beatrice
in glorious triumph to the heavenly spheres.

When each soul, dancing, had returned to that
position on the circle where it once had been,
all paused, like candles in a chandelier.

And in that flare which spoke to me at first,
I, hearing, sensed these words begin, smiling
as in their brilliance they became more pure.

'As I am here a mirror to the radiance
of everlasting light, so, looking back,
I grasp, in that, the wherefore of your thoughts.

You have your doubts. You want me to define –
with sharper and more open explanations,
directed at your human ear – the words

I uttered earlier: "Where all grow fat . . ."
and where I said: "No second ever rose."
We need to make distinctions as to that.

The providence that rules the universe,
in counsels so profound that all created
countenance will yield before it finds its depth,

intended that the Bride of Christ (He wooed her
with His sacred blood, His cries raised high)
should go to her Belovèd in delight,

sure of herself and truer still to Him,
and so ordained two princes that, on either side,
should walk along with her and be her guide.

The one was seraph-like in burning love,
the other in intelligence a splendour
on the earth that shone like Heaven's cherubim.

I'll speak of one. For – take whichever man –
in prizing him, you'll praise the other, too.
Their different actions served a single plan.

Between the Tupin and the stream that runs
down from the hill that saintly Ubald chose,
a fertile slope hangs off that mountainside

from which Perugia, through its Sun Gate, feels
both heat and chill. Behind that ridge, weeping,
are Nòcera and Gualdo, bowed by wind and shade.

And where its swiftest incline crashes down,
another sun was born to light the world –
as our sun ranges, sometimes, from the Ganges.

Let those, inventing words to suit that place,
not voice "Assisi" as "Ascesi" or "Arisen"
(*these* words all want) but properly the "Orient".

Nor was he far from his own rising dawn
when he began to make his country feel,
by his true powers, a certain strengthening.

Headlong he ran – a callow boy – to war
and fought, against his father, for a girl
to whom – as though to death – all lock joy's door.

So, *coram patre* in the bishop's court,
he joined himself with her and, ever on,
from day to day he loved her all the more.

She, sad and widowed of her first beloved,
remained a thousand years (and more) till he
came on to her – obscure, undated, scorned.

Nor did it count to hear how Caesar – terror
of the world – had found her true, unwavering,
with Amyclas, not moved by his command.

Nor did it count to hear that, likewise, she,
so fierce, so constant, wept (Mary herself
remained below) with Christ upon his Cross.

But lest in what I say I prove unclear,
then understand, in all I've just poured out,
this loving pair are Francis and pure Poverty.

The harmony, the looks of happiness
between these two, their tenderness and care,
their love, so wonderstruck, became the cause

of holy thoughts in Bernard (now revered),
the first who flung his shoes away and raced –
running, he thought himself too slow – for peace.

Such rampant goodness, riches yet untold!
Egidio flung his shoes away, Sylvester his,
chasing the groom, the bride so pleased them all.

So off he goes, Saint Francis, father, lord.
His bride was Poverty, his family these –
their waists already bound with simple cord.

Nor in abjection did it weigh his brows
to be Pietro Bernadone's kid,
nor when, amazingly, he faced disdain.

Rather, in sovereign manner he revealed
his stern intention to Pope Innocent,
who granted this devotion its first seal.

And when his little pauper-company
had grown (the wonder of his life would sound
far more when sung in glory in the skies),

this archimandrite in his holy will
was crowned now with a second diadem,
breathed by Eternal Spirit through Honorius.

Then after, thirsting for a martyr's fate,
he preached (before the Sultan's prideful throne)
his faith in Christ and all who followed him,

but found these people loath and far too sour
to change their ways. So, not to wait in vain,
he soon returned, to tend Italian vines.

A rough crag splits the Arno's course from Tiber.
There Francis took from Christ the final seal,
and on his limbs for two years bore that sign.

And when the one who'd dealt him so much good
was pleased to draw him up to that reward
which Francis earned through his great lowliness,

he then bestowed his *donna*, held so dear,
on followers and brothers, his true heirs,
commanding them, in faith, to love her well.

And from her bosom this illustrious soul
then chose to part, returning to his realm,
and chose no other bier for his own corpse.

Think of the other now, what *he* was like
if fit to work with Francis and maintain
the Ship of Peter on its rightful track.

Such was our patriarch, Saint Dominic.
And those who follow him as he commands
will bear, as you can tell, a precious freight.

But now this pastor's flock turns ravenous
for weird new fodder, so they cannot fail
to scatter wide through many different leas.

The further – wilful, wandering and wild –
his sheep desert him, so the emptier
they are of milk, returning to the fold.

It's true that some are fearful of such harm,
huddling against their shepherd still. They're few.
There's not much cloth now needed for their cowls.

Now if my words in meaning aren't too faint,
if you have been attentive, hearing them,
if you call what's been said to mind once more,

in part what you desire will be content.
You'll see why that firm plant is torn to shreds,
and see the strict correction that contends:

"Where all grow fat that do not go astray."'

Canto XIV

Centre to circle or circle to centre:
water in a round container moves like that,
depending where the rim is struck, inside or out.

I utter here the instant thought that chanced
across my mind when now, in all its glory,
the life of Thomas Aquinas fell silent,

born from a close resemblance that arose
between his words and these that, after him,
were voiced by Beatrice. She began:

'This man still needs – although he does not say,
nor is he even thinking it as yet –
to trace another truth down to its root.

Tell him: that light in which, as what you are,
your being in its substance is in-flowered,
will that remain eternally with you?

And if it does remain, then tell him how,
when once you are remade as visibles,
it cannot spoil your eyesight, being so.'

Compare: as dancers – wheeling, drawn and pressed
by keener happiness at certain points –
exult in voice, their gestures quickening,

so now, to hear her prompt, devoted prayer,
the holy circles showed new joy, in turns
of flashing speed and notes to wonder at.

Whoever mourns to think we here must die,
to live our lives up there, has never seen
the cool refreshment of the eternal shower.

The one and two and three who always lives
and always reign in three and two and one,
uncircumscribed and circumscribing all,

   had, three times now, been lauded in the songs
of every spirit there, the melody
a condign prize, however great the worth.

   Then, in the holiest of lights among
the lesser ring, I heard a voice (as modest
as, maybe, the angel's to Maria),

   answering: 'As long as this great festival
of Paradise goes on, so, too, our love
will cast these robes in rays around us all.

   That brightness follows from their inward fire,
that fire from vision. And their sight extends
as far as each, beyond their due, has grace.

   But when the glorious and sacred flesh
is clothing us once more, our person then
will be – complete and whole – more pleasing still.

   For then whatever has been granted us,
by utmost good, of free and gracious light
(the light through which we see Him) will increase.

   Hence, as must be, our seeing will increase,
increasing, too, the fire that vision lights,
the ray increasing that proceeds from that.

   But just as burning coal may give out flames,
yet overcome these with its own white light,
keeping, within, its shape and semblance whole,

   so, too, the shining-out that rings us round
will, in appearance, be surpassed by flesh
which all day long the earth now covers up.

Nor can it be that so much light will tire.
Our organs, physically, will have the strength
for every pleasure that can come to us.'

So ready and alert they seemed to me –
those double choirs – to add their plain 'Amen'
they showed their keen desire for long dead bones,

not only for themselves but for their mums,
their fathers, too, and others dear to them,
before they were these sempiternal flames.

Look! Round those circles, matched in clarity,
a lustre, more than what was there, was born,
as though a new horizon, brightening.

When early evening hours are drawing in,
new things begin to show across the sky
so that the sight both seems and seems not true.

There, too, it seemed to me that newer things
began to rise to view and form a ring
beyond the circumscription of those two.

True spark shower flying from the Holy Breath!
How suddenly it flared, how incandescent!
My eyes, defeated, could not bear the sight.

But Beatrice showed herself to me –
laughing, so beautiful she must be left
among things seen that memory can't pursue.

And so my eyes, regaining their right strength,
lifted once more. I saw myself alone,
borne with my lady to a higher good.

Seeing the flares of laughter in that star,
which seemed now far more fiery than before,
I knew full well that I'd been lifted higher.

With all my heart and with that tongue – flaming
alike in all our thoughts – aflame, I made to God
burnt offerings that befitted this new grace.

Nor had the ardour of that sacrifice
been drained still from my heart before it was,
I knew, propitious and acceptable.

For shining so – a ruby in its hue –
splendour appeared to me in two crossed rays.
'Eliosun!' I said. 'You grant this accolade.'

The galaxy, distinctly marked by lights,
both great and small, between the earth's two poles,
glistens and makes the learnèd wonder why.

So too, like constellations in the depths
of Mars, these rays composed the honoured sign
that quadrants (joined within a circle) form.

And here remembering surpasses skill:
that cross, in sudden flaring, blazed out Christ
so I can find no fit comparison.

But those who take their cross and follow Christ
will let me off where, wearily, I fail,
seeing in that white dawn, as lightning, Christ.

From horn to horn, from summit down to base,
there moved here scintillating points of light,
bright as their paths met, bright in passing on.

So minute specks of matter can be seen –
renewing how they look at every glance,
straight in their track, oblique, long, short, swift, slow –

moving through sunbeams that will sometimes streak
the shade that people, to protect themselves,
have won through their intelligence or art.

As harp or viol – in tempered harmony,
their many strings stretched tight – still ring and sing,
even to those who do not catch the tune,

so, though I did not understand their hymn,
an air now gathered that enraptured me
from lights appearing there throughout the cross.

I realized full well it sang high praise
for, as to one who does not understand
yet hears, there came to me, 'Rise up!' and 'Win!'

At which, I sank so deep in love of this
that never till that time had anything
entrammelled me in such delightful bonds.

These words of mine may seem perhaps too bold,
slighting the pleasure of those lovely eyes,
in which, when gazing, my desires all rest.

Whoever thinks, though, that the living prints
of every beauty grow the more they rise,
and notices I did not turn to these,

will make excuse for what I here confess
to win excuse, and see me speak the truth.
Holy delight is not excluded here.

Rather, in rising it will grow more pure.

Canto XVII

As Phaeton once, approaching Clymene,
to know for sure that news about himself
which still makes fathers chary of their sons,

so was I, too – and so was understood
by Beatrice and that holy lamp
which had, because of me, first left its place.

At which my lady said: 'Send out the flare
of your desire, as clear in coming forth
as, inwardly, the fire is stamped in you,

not to increase, by saying what that is,
the knowledge we already have, but more,
to find, when speaking out, we slake your thirst.'

'You, the dear soil in which I thrive. You so
on-high yourself that you see well (as sure
as mortals know, in triangles, two angles

aren't obtuse) contingencies before
they come to be, your eye set wondering on
the point at which all times are present time.

While I was still in Virgil's company,
climbing the hill that remedies our souls,
so, too, descending to the dead, waste world,

he spoke to me in grave and weighty words
about my future life, so I should feel
four-square against the blows that were to come.

I'd therefore willingly receive sure words
that told what fortune now draws near to me.
Those arrows that we know will come fly slower.'

I said all this to that same light that, first,
had spoken out to me, and thus confessed,
as Beatrice wished, what I desired.

Not in those enigmatic words that once
entrammelled pagan fools, like birds in lime,
before the Lamb of God bore off their sin,

but clear, precise and solemn in his speech,
that father-love now gave me his reply,
enclosed, yet shown, in his own laughing light.

'Contingency, whose sphere does not extend
beyond the margins of your earthly things,
is framed and painted in eternal sight.

This does not, though, imply necessity,
except, as might be when some glass reflects
a ship swept onward by a raging stream.

From that same view there comes before my eyes
(as to the ear sweet melodies may come)
the time that now prepares itself for you.

As once Hippolytus was driven out
of Athens by his father's wife, perverse
and pitiless, so you'll leave Florence, too.

This much is willed, this much already sought.
And soon he'll see it through, who thinks it up,
where all day long Christ's self is bought and sold.

Shrill cries of blame will chase the ones who lose –
they always do. But vengeance, when it falls,
will speak of that same Truth that deals it out.

You'll leave behind you all you hold most dear.
And this will be the grievous arrow barb
that exile, first of all, will shoot your way.

And you will taste the saltiness of bread
when offered by another's hand – as, too,
how hard it is to climb a stranger's stair.

Yet what will weigh upon your shoulders worst
is all the foul, ill-minded company
that you, in that dark vale, will fall to keep.

For that ungrateful, crazy, vicious crew
will turn as one against you. Yet it's them
whose brows before too long will blush with shame.

Their deeds will prove what animals they are.
And so much so, the finer course for you
would be to form a party on your own.

Your refuge and your safe abode will be
the courtesy at first of that great Lombard
whose blazon is a stair and holy bird.

And he will hold you in such high regard
that "ask" and "do" between the two of you
will place as first what others put behind.

You'll see, along with him, his brother, too,
so strongly marked, when he was born, by Mars
that all his deeds will prove remarkable.

People as yet know nothing of this man.
He is still fresh and young. The astral wheels
have worked around him for a mere nine years.

Before the Gascon tricks great Henry, though,
the sparks of his high virtue will appear,
scornful of silver and the toils of war.

His proud liberality will make its mark,
and even enemies, in seeing that,
will have no power to mute their tongues in praise.

Await him, and the good he'll bring to you.
By him a multitude will be transformed,
the poor exalted and the rich brought low.

Now carry, written in your memory
(don't speak!), report of him.' He then said things
that even witnesses will not believe.

He added, then: 'It was of this, dear son,
they spoke. These are the wiles and snares that lie
concealed by some few circlings of the stars.

Yet I'd not have you envy those around.
Your life and fame en-futures far beyond
the punishment their perfidy receives.'

Now falling silent, that most sacred soul
declared his hand unburdened of the thread
of that taut weave which I had stretched for him.

So I began – as anyone in doubt
goes on and craves good counsel from the one
who sees, whose will is right, whose love is strong.

'I now see clearly, Father, how the years spur down
on me – and how the blow they mean to strike
is worse to those who, fleeing, flinch aside.

It's better, then, I arm myself with foresight,
so if that dearest place is snatched away,
my verses do not lose me all the rest.

Down through the world of endless bitterness,
around the mountain where my lady's look
raised me so I could reach its lovely peak,

then through these heavenly spheres, from light to light
I've learnt of things which, if I now repeat,
will leave in many mouths an acid taste.

   And if I prove a timid friend to truth
I shall, I fear, forego my life among
those souls who'll count as ancient our own time.'

   The light in which the treasure I found there
was smiling still, first blazed in corruscations
as will a ray of sun in golden mirrors,

   and then replied: 'All murky consciences,
who feel their own or any other's shame
are bound to baulk at your abrasive words.

   But none the less, all lies put clean aside,
make plain what in your vision you have seen,
and let them scratch wherever they may itch.

   For if at first your voice tastes odious,
still it will offer, as digestion works,
life-giving nutriment to those who eat.

   The words you shout will be like blasts of wind
that strike the very summit of the trees.
And this will bring no small degree of fame.

   For you've been shown in all these circling wheels –
around the mountain, in the sorrowing vale –
only those souls whose fame is widely known,

   since those who hear you speak will never pause
or give belief to any instances
whose family roots are hidden or unknown,

   nor demonstrations that remain obscure.'

Canto XXIII

Compare: a bird, among her well-loved boughs,
has rested all night long while things lie hid,
poised where her dear brood sleeps within their nest;

and then, to glimpse the looks she's longed to see,
and find the food her fledglings feed upon
(these efforts weigh with her as pure delight)

before dawn comes she mounts an open sprig,
and there, her heart ablaze, awaits the sun,
eyes sharpening, fixed, till day is truly born.

So, too, head raised, tall, straight, my *donna* stood,
attention wholly on that stretch of sky
where, under noon, the sun displays least speed.

And I, to see her stand enraptured so,
became like one desiring still what he
has not – and yet in hope is satisfied.

But little time went by between these two –
I mean my waiting, and my seeing now
the skies that, brightening still, grew yet more bright.

And 'Look!' said Beatrice. 'Triumphing,
the soldiery of Christ, and all the yield,
brought from the orbit of the farthest spheres!'

Her face, it seemed to me, now burned so bright,
her eyes so filled with utmost happiness,
that I must needs pass on and frame no word.

As in the calm, clear skies of moonlit nights,
tri-form Diana smiles (eternal nymphs,
around her, paint all Heaven's curving spheres),

above a thousand lanterns or still more,
I saw one sun that, soaring, lit them all,
as our sun lights the stars seen over us.

And through this clear and living light there shone
the being that creates that glow, too bright
within my eyes for me to tolerate.

My sweetness! Beatrice, guiding me!
She spoke: 'This power that overcomes your sight
is one from which no shelter can be sought.

Here is all wisdom, and the strength that cleared
the open road that runs from Heaven to earth,
for which so long was once such deep desire.'

As bolts of fire, unlocked from thunder clouds,
expand beyond containment in those bounds,
then fall to ground (as fire, by nature, can't),

so, too, surrounded by this solemn feast,
my own mind, grown the greater now, went forth
and can't remember what it then became.

'Open your eyes and look at what I am!
You have seen things by which you're made so strong,
you can, now, bear to look upon my smile.'

I was like one whose waking sense returns
yet strives in vain – his dreaming now oblivion –
to bring once more that vision back to mind,

as I now heard that utterance which deserves
a gratitude that never should be dimmed
from that great book that tells of things long past.

Even if all those voices were to sound
that Polyhymnia and her sister muses
fed on their sweetest milk so richly once,

and aid me, singing of that holy smile
and how her holy look grew purer still,
I'd still not reach one thousandth of the truth.

And so, imagining this Paradise,
the sacred epic has to make a leap,
as when we find the road ahead cut off.

Yet no one if they've gauged that weighty theme –
and seen what mortal shoulders bear the load –
would criticize such trembling backing-out.

The waves that my adventurous prow here cleaves
are no mere sea-loch that some skiff might cross,
or helmsmen lacking in the proper skill.

'Why is it that my face in-loves you so
that you don't turn to see the garden where,
beneath Christ's rays, such beauty is en-flowered?

The rose in which the Word of God became
our flesh is here. And here those *fleurs-de-lys*
whose perfume marks the path we rightly tread.'

So, Beatrice. And I, quick to read
whatever she might counsel, gave myself
to battle, feeble though my eyelids were.

My eyes have seen at times – though wrapped in shade –
a ray of limpid sunlight, filtering
through broken cloud, across a field of flowers.

So here I saw a swirling crowd of splendours
flung out like thunderbolts down burning beams,
and could not see from where these flashes came.

You, Generous Strength! You leave your imprint here.
To open this arena to my eyes (powerless
to see You otherwise) You rose on high.

The naming of that lovely flower which I,
at dawn and evening, call upon, compelled
my mind to face in full the greatest fire.

And as my eyes, together, now portrayed
the scope and nature of that bright, live star,
victorious there, victorious here below,

straight through the skies another torch came down
spun in a circle, as a crown might be,
and formed a ring around her, turning there.

The sweetest melody that sounds on earth,
or that which most attracts the soul to it,
would seem like cloud ripped wide by thunder claps

when heard beside the sounding of that lyre
whose notes now crowned the lovely sapphire-stone,
through whom the skies en-sapphire clearer still.

'I am the angel-love called Gabriel,
encircling here the height of joy that breathes
around the womb our Longed-for sheltered in.

Lady of Heaven, I shall spin these turns
till, in procession, you, behind your son,
make the High Sphere, on entering, more divine.'

And so the perfect circling of that tune
sealed its conclusion, while the other lights
rang out the sound of Maria's name.

The regal surcoat of those rolling spheres
that form our universe, alive with stars,
all shimmering at the breathing of God's rule

now stretched its inner shore so far above
that nothing of it showed from where I was,
no glimpse of that First Mover came to view.

Therefore my eyes could not command the power
to follow as that flame, within its crown,
rose up so close behind the seed she'd borne.

A baby, suckling, once it's full of milk,
will hold its arms out wide towards its mum
to make known outwardly its inner flame.

So, at their incandescent peaks, these gleams
stretched up. And this, to me, made clear what depths
of heartfelt love they bore towards Maria.

But all remained there, still within my sight,
singing in such sweet tones '*Regina coeli*'
delight at that will never leave my heart.

What richness, what abundance now well-stored
within such overflowing barns – which were
good husbandmen who sowed the seed below.

Here life is lived rejoicing in that hoard,
gained ever weeping in the exile years
of Babylon, when gold was put aside.

And here beneath the most exalted Son
of God and Mary, in His victory,
with all the new and all the ancient court,

triumphs the one who holds such glory's key.

Canto XXVII

'To Father and Son and the Holy Ghost,
glory on high!' all Heaven here began,
till I, at that sweet song, reeled drunkenly.

And what I saw, it seemed, was now the laughter
of the universe. So drunkenness, for me,
came in through hearing and, no less, through sight.

The joy of that! The happiness beyond all words!
A life of peace and love, entire and whole!
Riches all free of craving, troubleless!

The faces of the four before my eyes
were bright with fire. That soul (the first who came)
began to grow more brilliant still at this.

And now, in how it looked, this face became
what Jove would be if he and Mars were birds,
and both exchanged their plumage, white for red.

The providence that makes division here
of duties, tasks and offices imposed
a perfect silence on the holy choir.

And then I heard: 'If I change colour now,
don't be amazed at that. For all of these,
as I go on, you'll see change colour, too.

He who on earth has robbed me of my place,
my place, my place – which therefore, in the sight
of God's dear Son, stands vacant now – has made

of my own burial ground a shit hole
reeking of blood and pus. In this the sod

who fell from here down there takes sheer delight.'

With that same colour that a cloud takes on,
morning or evening, when it meets the sun,
I saw, in every part, the heavens flush.

And as some innocent – herself quite clean
in conscience – when she notes another's fault
may still, on hearing this, grow chaste and shy,

so Beatrice changed in countenance.
So, too, I think the heavens were once eclipsed
when Utmost Power submitted to the Cross.

And then Saint Peter's words went on, his voice
transformed so utterly from what it was
that he, in look, could not have been more changed.

'The Bride of Christ was not brought forth and raised
on blood of mine – of Linus, too, and Cletus –
to be made use of in pursuit of gold,

but rather, to pursue here living joy,
Sixtus and Pius, Urban, Calixtus,
after harsh tears all shed their blood for this.

We did not mean that some of Christ's own race
should sit in favour on our heirs' right hand,
and others, to the left, incur disgrace;

nor that the keys entrusted to my hands
should serve as battle emblem on the flag
that fought against those marked by baptism;

nor that, myself, I should become the stamp
that seals the sale of untrue privilege.
I flare and redden often at this thought.

Down there, in every pasture, ravening wolves
are seen dressed up as shepherds and as priests.

God our defence, why are you still unmoved?

Gascons along with bankers from Cahors
prepare themselves to drink our martyr blood.
To what corrupted ends good starts may sink!

But Providence on high that made defence
through Scipio at Rome of this world's fame
will soon, as I conceive it, offer aid.

And you, my son, whose body weighs you down
so you'll return below, speak openly
and do not hide what I don't hide from you.'

When Sun and Goat Horn touch as winter signs,
the air in our terrestrial atmosphere
floats down in falls of frozen vapour flakes.

So now I saw, with *upward* sweeping flakes,
the aether decked in those triumphant airs
that first had passed their time with us below.

My eyes, in following these semblances,
followed until the space between became
so great it took away sight's power to pass.

At which my lady, seeing me absolved
from all attention to the heights, now said:
'Now sink your gaze, and see how far you've turned.'

I saw that since the time I'd first looked down
I'd moved in those six hours through all the arc,
mid-point to end, the first zone makes on earth,

so that I saw, beyond Cadiz, the mad
sea-jaunt of Ulysses and, east, the shore
where soft Europa once was borne away.

And more still of that eastward threshing floor
would have been shown me but, beneath my feet,

the sun, processing, reached a farther sign.

My mind, so deep in love that always woos,
as *donna*, my *donna*, burned more fiercely still
to turn its eyes once more to where she was.

Though art or nature, to possess our minds,
may, in its paintings or in flesh itself,
produce beguiling pastures for our eyes,

these all would seem as nothing when compared
with that divine delight which shone on me
when I turned round to see her smiling look.

The inward powers her glance bestowed on me,
uprooting me from Leda's lovely nest,
impelled me to the swiftest of the skies.

Its regions so exalted, living bright,
are all so uniform I cannot say
which Beatrice chose to be my place.

But she, who saw the strength of my desire,
laughing with such great happiness
that God appeared rejoicing in her face:

'The order in the natural spheres that stills
the central point and moves, round that, all else,
here sets its confine and begins its rule.

This primal sphere has no "where" other than
the mind of God. The love that makes it turn
is kindled there, so, too, the powers it rains.

Brightness and love contain it in one ring,
as this, in turn, contains the spheres below.
And only He who binds it knows the bond.

Its motion is not gauged by other marks.

All other marks are measured out from this –
as ten is factored by its half and fifth.

   So now it will be clear to you how Time
takes root within the humus of this bowl,
and shows its fronds in every other part.

   Crass, itching greed! You plunge our mortal sense
so far within your depth that none can drag
their eyes above the mounting turbulence!

   Intention blossoms well in human hearts.
But rain, unending rain, will render down
the true, ripe plum to shrivelled pods of blight.

   Good faith and innocence are only found
in infant schools. And both will long have fled
before the cheek is covered with a beard.

   There's one kid, burbling still, awaiting food,
who when he's fluent in his speech will gorge
on every dish, beneath whatever moon.

   There's one there (burbling, too) who loves his mum
and heeds her words, who, when his tongue grows whole,
will long to see her buried in her grave.

   And so the whitest skin is scorched pitch black
merely to glimpse the lovely child of him
who brings the dawn and leaves behind the dark.

   And you – so you should not suppose this strange –
think that on earth there's no one who will rule,
and so the human family goes astray.

   But those neglected hundredths in our dates
will make of January a spring-song month
before these circling heights send down such rays

that storms of fortune, so long waited for,
will spin the stern to where the prow is now,
so all the fleet will run a proper course,
  and fruit will follow truly from the flower.'

Canto XXX

Maybe, around six thousand miles away,
the sixth hour, close to noon, flares out, while earth
inclines its shadow-cone to rest, near level.

At this same time, the mid-point of the sky
will start, so deep above us, to transform,
and some stars lose their semblance in those depths.

Then brightest Aurora who serves the sun
advances and, dawning, the skies, vista
by vista, are closed till even the loveliest is gone.

In this way, too, the victories that play
for ever round the point that conquered me –
enclosed, it seems, by that which they enclose –

was, little by little, quenched before my gaze.
And so, from seeing nothing – and in love –
I turned my eyes towards Beatrice.

If all that has, till this, been said of her
were now enclosed to form one word of praise,
it would not, even so, fulfil my need.

The beauty I saw, transcending every kind,
is far beyond us here – nor only us.
Its maker, I think, alone could know its joy.

From now on, I'll admit, I'm overwhelmed,
defeated worse than all before – in comic
or in tragic genre – by what my theme demands.

As sunlight trembles in enfeebled eyes,
calling to mind how sweet to me her smile was,
itself deprives my mind of memory.

Not since the day that I, in our first life,
first saw her face until this living sight,
has song in me been cut so cleanly short.

It is, however, right that I stand down –
as every artist, at the utmost, does –
and no more trace her beauty, forming verse.

And so what then she was I now will leave
to clarions far greater than my trumpet sounds,
and draw my vaunting line towards its end.

As she then was – a guide in word and deed,
her work all done – she spoke again: 'We've left
the greatest of material spheres, rising

to light, pure light of intellect, all love,
the love of good in truth, all happiness,
a happiness transcending every rapture.

Here you will see the two great heavenly ranks,
angels and saints – the saints in countenance
as you, on Judgement Day, will see them stand.'

As lights, when flashing suddenly, disperse
the spirits of the retina, and rob
the eye of seeing even strong, bright things,

so, bright around me, shone a living light
that left me, baby-like, in swaddling weaves
of brilliance, so that nothing showed to me.

'The love that gives this Heaven its quietness
will always make its saving welcome thus,
to form a candle ready for its flame.'

No sooner had these brief words entered me
than I rose up – as truly I could tell –

above the summit of my natural powers.

New seeing-strength I kindled in myself,
so that no light, however crystalline,
could cause my eyes to close in self-defence.

I saw light form a river in full spate,
fire-dazzle-gilded, flowing through verges
painted afresh in colours of wonderful spring.

And rising from that flood, alive, were sparks
that everywhere alighted on the flowers,
like rubies set in gold encirclements –

then all, as though the perfumes made them drunk,
plunged in that swirling miracle once more.
And yet where one sank in, still more spun out.

'The fine desire that fires and urges you
to gain still fuller news of all you see,
delights me more, the more the longing swells.

And yet before your thirst is satisfied,
you'll need to drink these waters to the full.'
Those words were hers, the sunlight of my eyes.

Then following: 'The river and the glint
of topaz, in and out, the smile of grass – these all are
shadowed prefaces that hint at their own truth.

That does not mean that any is, itself,
unripe, acid or green. The lack is yours.
Your sight as yet cannot move proudly on.'

No baby, waking later from its nap
than normally it would, so hurled itself
face down to mother's milk as I did now.

To make my eyes, as mirrors, better still,

I bent towards the wave that, flowing there,
will sweep us always onward to in-bettering.

   I drank to the arching eaves of my brow,
and then saw all anew, as though that length
of light had now, in form, become a round.

   If masqueraders, hidden in their veils,
undress those features (not their own) in which
they'd vanished once, their look seems somehow changed.

   So now, it seemed, these flowers and flecks of light
altered, to join and celebrate still more.
And I saw, now made known, both heavenly courts.

   Splendour of God! Through you I came to see
triumph exalting in the realm of truth.
Grant me true strength to say what then I saw.

   There is, above us there, a light that makes
the All-Creator in creation seen
by those who only seeing Him have peace.

   This light became a circle in its form,
extending its circumference so far
as might a belt too generous round the sun.

   All that appears is made there by a ray
reflected from the curve of that First Sphere
which draws its life and movings from that light.

   It is as though the incline of some hill
were mirrored in a lake below, as if
to view itself adorned in flower and richest green.

   Above that light, and standing round, I saw
a thousand tiers or more as mirrorings
of those of ours who've now returned up there.

Imagine, when the least of all these grades
could gather to itself so great a light,
how great the wealth is at the rose's fringe.

My eyes, despite such breadth and altitude,
were not confused or blurred but took all in –
the kind and sum of this light-heartedness.

Nothing's gained here or lost by 'near' and 'far'.
For where God rules without some means between,
the law of nature bears no weight at all.

Into the gold of that now-always rose,
which grows from arc to arc, dilates and breathes
the scent of praise to always-springtime Sun,

she drew me – Beatrice – like someone
yearning, while silent, to say: 'The wonder!
Look there, how great this white-caped gathering is!

Our city, look! And see how wide it sweeps.
The honoured places – look! – they're almost full,
and few we long to see are still to come.

Your eyes are fixed upon a single throne,
drawn by the crown already set on that.
And long before you join this marriage feast,

the soul will sit – imperial in the world –
of noble Arrigo, who came to rule
an Italy unready for him yet.

The blind cupidity bewitching you
has made you all akin to little brats
who – famished, dying – still beat off their nurse.

And in the Sacred Forum one presides
whose public and whose covert deeds will not

accord or travel in a single groove.

But not for long. God will not suffer him
to keep that sacred role. He'll soon be flung
where Simon Magus gets what he deserves.

The Anagnese Pope will sink still further down.'

Canto XXXII

Heart-whole in pleasure, the contemplative
freely took on himself the teacher's role,
beginning thus the holy words he spoke:
　'The gash that Mary healed and soothed with oil
was opened first, and then made worse, by her
who sits, so beautiful, at Mary's feet.
　Ranked in the order that the third thrones form,
below Eve, Rachel sits. And then along
from Rachel, as you see, is Beatrice.
　Sara, Rebecca, Judith and the one
who bore the mother of the man who sang,
mourning his fault, the "*Miserere mei*".
　Descending step to step, you see all these
as I, in giving each her name, proceed,
now travelling down this rose from leaf to leaf.
　And downward from the seventh of these tiers
(as down to that) the Hebrew women come,
dividing all the curls within that flower.
　And these (according to the way their faith
in Christ looked back or forth) here form the wall
that separates the sacred steps in two.
　On that side, where the flower is fully grown,
with all its petals at their full extent,
sit those who showed belief in Christ to come.
　There on the other side, where unfilled space
still intersects the hemispheres, are those
who turned their countenance to Christ now come.

And where, on this side, there's the glorious throne
of Heaven's own Lady and, below, those seats
that, under hers, divide the rose in two,

so, too, across from that, there sits great John.
That saint bore desert and cruel martyrdom,
then, after – till Christ came – two years in Hell;

And under him, elected to divide,
Saint Francis, Benedict, Augustine, too,
with others down to here, from rank to rank.

Look up in wonder at God's providence.
He'll fill this garden to the same extent
with those who kept the faith in these two ways.

Know, too, that from the rung that, midway, strikes
the line that marks these two divisions off,
no one will sit by merit of their own –

of others, rather, where conditions hold.
For all of these are spirits loosed from earth
before they, truly, could conceive free choice.

And this, if you will look and listen hard,
will be entirely clear to you. Just note
their faces. Hear, as well, their children-voice.

Now you're in doubt and, doubting, do not speak.
But I shall disentangle this tight knot,
which your own subtle reasonings have tied.

Within the broad expanse of all this realm
there cannot be a single point that's chance,
nor any hunger, thirst or misery.

For all that you may see is here decreed
by God's eternal law. Hence, right and fit,
all corresponds as finger to a ring.

And so it is that, not without good cause,
these children – sped too soon to this true life –
are in their excellences less and more.

The king, through whom this kingdom is at peace,
in such great love, and in such pure delight,
that nothing in our wills dare aim so high,

creating, in his look of happiness,
all minds, bestowed, as he best pleased, his grace
in different ways. The outcome says enough.

And this, expressed and clear in Holy Writ,
is noted in the case of those two twins
who, in their mother's womb, were moved to wrath.

It follows from the colour of their hair
to what degree of grace the highest light
encrowns most fittingly the head of each.

Therefore, with no regard to how they act,
these are placed here in differing degrees
by difference only of their first sharp sight.

In earliest times, it used to be enough,
to gain salvation, that with innocence
parental faith alone should be conjoined.

Then, when these early epochs were complete,
all males were circumcised to win them powers
appropriate to their wings of innocence.

But, later, when the age of grace arrived,
such innocence – when baptism in Christ
was not fulfilled – was bound on Hell's first rim.

Return now. See that face resembling Christ
closer than all. For that bright light alone
can make you wholly fit to look on Christ.'

I saw such happiness rain down on her,
borne by those holy intellects – made first
to fly with wings across that heavenly height –

that nothing I had ever seen before
had brought my wondering eyes to such a poise,
nor shown so much to me of how God looks.

And that first angel-love, descending there,
was singing – wings extended in her sight –
'Ave Maria gratia plena'.

There answered this the sacred cantilene
from every region of the happy court.
At which, their faces showed the more serene.

'O holy father, who for me could bear
to be down here and leave that lovely place
where, as eternally decreed, you sit,

which is that angel who, with such delight,
looks at our Queen and gazes in her eyes
so deep in love he seems to be on fire?'

I went, in this way, back to learn from him
of one who drew his beauty from Maria,
as, from the sun, the morning star draws light.

'All prowess, charm and elegance of heart
as may appear in angels or men's souls
is found in him, and we all wish it so.

For he it is who carried down the palm
to Mary when the only Son of God
chose to take on the weight of human form.

But come now, note and follow with your eyes,
as I go speaking, all the noble sires
of this supremely true imperium.

These two who sit above – the happiest,
in being nearest to the Empress throne –
are as the double root-stock of this rose.

He who sits next in justice, to her left,
is that first father through whose reckless taste
the human species tasted so much gall.

There on the right you see the honoured sire
of Holy Church to whom Christ left in trust
the keys to this most delicate of flowers.

And he who saw, before he came to die,
the heavy times of that beloved bride,
first won upon the Cross with lance and nails,

sits next to him, and next to him now rests
that lord beneath whose guidance there once lived
a race ungrateful, shifting, obstinate.

Across from Peter, as you see, sits Anne,
so happy as she wonders at her child
she does not move her eyes to sing "Hosannah".

And facing Adam, father of our tribe,
Lucia sits. When you, in ruin, bent your brows,
Lucia moved that *donna* to your aid.

But since your time of slumber races by,
at this point we shall end, as tailors do –
who skilfully make skirts from little cloth.

And turn your eyes towards the Primal Love,
so that, in looking there, your eye should pierce
as far as possible His dazzling light.

But lest it be, perhaps, on your frail wings,
thinking you rise beyond, you sink back down,
it's best that, praying for the gift of grace,

you beg for grace from her who can assist.
And here you'll follow me with such good heart
that from my words your feelings won't depart.'
  And so he now began his holy prayer.

Canto XXXIII

'Virgin and mother, daughter of your son,
greater than all in honour and humility,
you are the point that truth eternally

is fixed upon. And you have made the nature
of the human being proud. Its maker, then,
did not disdain to make himself his making.

Love, in your womb, was fanned to fire again.
And here, in this eternal peace, the warmth of love
has brought the Rose to germinate and bloom.

You are, for us, the noon-time torch of love.
You are, among those mortals there below,
the clearest fountain of their living hopes.

You are, in dignity and power, Our Lady.
All who, in wanting grace, do not seek help
from you, might wish to soar yet lack the wings.

Nor in your kindness do you give your aid
to those alone who ask, but often run,
before they ask, to them in generous freedom.

In you is pity, in you compassion,
in you all-giving power. All good in you
is gathered up that creature form can bear.

This man is one who, from the deepest void
in all the universe, has seen thus far,
and one by one, all lives in spirit mode.

To you, a suppliant, he comes, and asks
that, by your grace, he gains the strength to rise
in sight more still to greet the final peace.

I never burned for visions of my own
more than I do that he might see. To you
I offer all my prayers – praying my prayers
   are not too few – that you should free this man
from all the clouds of his mortality,
so highest happiness be shown to him.

   Our Queen, to you, who may do what you will,
I also pray you keep him (he has seen
so much!) healthy in all his heart intends.

   Watch, and defeat the impulses of man.
See! Beatrice with so many saints
closes her hands in prayers along with mine.'

   The eyes – which God both loves and venerates –
attentive to these orisons, made clear
how welcome to her were these holy prayers

   and then turned straight to the eternal light
in which (we're bound to think) no creature's eye
inwardly travels with such clarity.

   And drawing nearer, as I had to now,
the end of all desires, in my own self
I ended all the ardour of desire.

   Now Bernard, smiling, made a sign to me
that I look up. Already, though, I was,
by my own will, as he desired I be.

   My sight, becoming pure and wholly free,
entered still more, then more, along the ray
of that one light which, of itself, is true.

   Seeing, henceforward, was far more than speech –
yielding before the sight I saw – can show.
Mind's memory yields, outraged at that beyond.

Like those who see so clearly while they dream
that marks of feeling, when their dreaming ends,
remain, though nothing more returns to mind,

so I am now. For nearly all I saw
has gone, even if, still, within my heart,
there drops the sweetness that was born from that.

So, too, in sunlight, snow will lose its seal.
So, too, the oracles the Sibyl wrote
on weightless leaves are lost upon the wind.

You raise yourself so far, O highest light,
above our dying thoughts! Now lend once more
some little part of what it seemed you were,

and make my tongue sufficient in its powers
that it may leave at least one telling spark
of all your glory to a future race.

Returning somewhat to my memory,
re-echoing a little in my verse,
your triumph over all will be more known.

As I believe, the sharp light I sustained
in that live ray was such that, if I'd turned
away, eyes blurring, I'd have lost my track.

And therefore (I remember this) I grew
the braver as I bore that light, and joined
the look I had to that unending might.

Grace, in all plenitude, you dared me set
my seeing eyes on that eternal light
so that all seeing there achieved its end.

Within in its depths, this light, I saw, contained,
bound up and gathered in a single book,
the leaves that scatter through the universe –

beings and accidents and modes of life,
as though blown all together in a way
that what I say is just a simple light.

This knotting-up of universal form
I saw, I'm sure of that. For now I feel,
in saying this, a gift of greater joy.

One single point in trauma is far more,
for me, than those millennia since sail
made Neptune marvel under Argos-shade.

And so my mind, held high above itself,
looked on, intent and still, in wondering awe
and, lit by wonder, always flared anew.

We all become, as that light strikes us, such
we cannot (this would be impossible)
consent to turn and seek some other face.

For good – the only object of our will –
is gathered up entire in that one light.
Outside it, all is flawed that's perfect there.

And now my spark of words will come more short –
even of what I still can call to mind –
than baby tongues still bathing in mum's milk.

But not because that living light on which,
in wonder, I now fixed my eyes showed more
than always as before and one sole sight.

Rather, as sight in me, yet looking on,
grew finer still, one single showing-forth
(me, changing mutely) laboured me more near.

Within the being – lucid, bright and deep –
of that high brilliance, there appeared to me
three circling spheres, three-coloured, one in span.

And one, it seemed, was mirrored by the next
twin rainbows, arc to arc. The third seemed fire,
and breathed to first and second equally.

How short mere speaking falls, how faint against
my own idea. And this idea, compared
to what I saw . . . well, 'little' hardly squares.

Eternal light, you sojourn in yourself alone.
Alone, you know yourself. Known to yourself,
you, knowing, love and smile on your own being.

An inter-circulation, thus conceived,
appears in you like mirrored brilliancy.
But when a while my eyes had looked this round,

deep in itself, it seemed – as painted now,
in those same hues – to show our human form
At which, my sight was set entirely there.

As some geometer may fix his mind
to find a circle-area, yet lack,
in thought, the principle his thoughts require,

likewise with me at this sight seen so new.
I willed myself to see what fit there was,
image to circle, and how this all in-where'd.

But mine were wings that could not rise to that,
save that, with this, my mind, was stricken through
by sudden lightning bringing what it wished.

All powers of high imagining here failed.
But now my will and my desire were turned,
as wheels that move in equilibrium,

by love that moves the sun and other stars.